HOW TO IMPROVE STUDENT LEARNING:
30 PRACTICAL IDEAS

如何提升学生的学习能力

（美）Richard Paul　（美）Linda Elder　著

外语教学与研究出版社
FOREIGN LANGUAGE TEACHING AND RESEARCH PRESS
北京 BEIJING

京权图字：01-2016-3326

图书在版编目（CIP）数据

如何提升学生的学习能力：英文／（美）保罗（Paul, R.），（美）埃尔德（Elder, L.）著. —— 北京：外语教学与研究出版社，2016.4（2016.6重印）

（思想者指南系列丛书）
ISBN 978-7-5135-7467-9

I. ①如… II. ①保… ②埃… III. ①学习方法－研究－英文 IV.
①G791

中国版本图书馆CIP数据核字(2016)第097131号

出 版 人　蔡剑峰
项目负责　任　佼
责任编辑　任　佼
封面设计　孙莉明
出版发行　外语教学与研究出版社
社　　址　北京市西三环北路19号（100089）
网　　址　http://www.fltrp.com
印　　刷　北京联兴盛业印刷股份有限公司
开　　本　850×1168　1/32
印　　张　2
版　　次　2016年5月第1版 2016年6月第2次印刷
书　　号　ISBN 978-7-5135-7467-9
定　　价　9.90元

购书咨询：（010）88819926　电子邮箱：club@fltrp.com
外研书店：https://waiyants.tmall.com
凡印刷、装订质量问题，请联系我社印制部
联系电话：（010）61207896　电子邮箱：zhijian@fltrp.com
凡侵权、盗版书籍线索，请联系我社法律事务部
举报电话：（010）88817519　电子邮箱：banquan@fltrp.com
法律顾问：立方律师事务所　刘旭东律师
　　　　　中咨律师事务所　殷　斌律师
物料号：274670001

序　言

　　思辨能力或者批判性思维由两个维度组成，在情感态度层面包括勤学好问、相信理性、尊重事实、谨慎判断、公正评价、敏于探究、持之以恒地追求真理等一系列思维品质或心理倾向；在认知层面包括对证据、概念、方法、标准、背景等要素进行阐述、分析、评价、推理与解释的一系列技能。

　　思辨能力的重要性应该是不言而喻的。两千多年前的中国古代典籍《礼记·中庸》曰："博学之，审问之，慎思之，明辨之，笃行之。"古希腊哲人苏格拉底说："未经审视的人生不值得一过。"可以说，文明的诞生正是人类自觉运用思辨能力，不断适应并改造自然环境的结果。如果说游牧时代、农业时代以及现代早期，人类思辨能力虽然并不完善，也远未普及，但通过科学技术以及人文知识的不断积累创新，推动人类文明阔步前进，已经显示出不可抑制的巨大能量，那么，进入信息时代、知识经济时代和全球化时代，思辨能力对于人类文明整体可持续发展以及对于每一个体的生存和发展，其重要性将史无前例地彰显。

　　我们已进入一个加速变化、普遍联系和日益复杂的时代。随着交通技术和信息技术日新月异的发展，不同国家和文化空前紧密地联系在一起。这在促进合作的同时，导致了更多的冲突；人类所掌握的技术力量与日俱增，在不断提高物质生活质量的同时，也极大地破坏了我们赖以生存的自然环境；工业化、城市化和信息化的不断延伸，全方位扩大了人的自由空间，同时却削弱了维系社会秩序和稳定的价值体系与行为准则。这一切变化对人类的思辨能力和应变能力都提出了前所未有的要求。正如本套丛书作者理查德·保罗（Richard Paul）和琳达·埃尔德（Linda Elder）所创办的思辨研究中心的"使命"所指出的,"我们身处其中的这个世界要求我们不断重新学习,习惯性重新思考我们的决定,周期性重新评价我们的工作和生活方式。简言之,我们面临一个全新的世界,在这个新世界,大脑掌控自己并经常进行自我分析的能力将日益决定我们工作的质量、生活的质量乃至我们的生存本身。"

遗憾的是,面临时代巨变对人类思辨能力提出的新挑战,我们的教育和社会都尚未做好充分准备。从小学到大学,在很大程度上我们的教育依然围绕知识的搬运而展开,学校周而复始的考试不断强化学生对标准答案的追求而不是对问题复杂性和探索过程的关注,全社会也尚未形成鼓励独立思辨与开拓创新的氛围。

我们知道,人类大脑并不具备天然遗传的思辨能力。事实上,在自然状态下,人们往往倾向于以自我为中心或随波逐流,容易被偏见左右,固守陈见,急于判断,为利益或情感所左右。因此,思辨能力需要通过后天的学习和训练得以提高,思辨能力培养也因此应该成为教育的不懈使命。

哈佛大学以培养学生"乐于发现和思辨"为根本追求;剑桥大学也把"鼓励怀疑精神"奉为宗旨。美国学者彼得·法乔恩(Peter Facione)一言以蔽之:"教育,不折不扣,就是学会思考。"

和任何其他技能的学习一样,学会思考也是有规律可循的。首先,学习者应该了解思辨的基本特点和理论框架。根据理查德·保罗和琳达·埃尔德的研究,所有的推理都有一个目的,都试图澄清或解决问题,都基于假设,都从某一视角展开,都基于数据、信息和证据,都通过概念和观念进行表达,都通过推理或阐释得出结论并对数据赋予意义,都会产生影响或后果。分析一个推理或论述的质量或有效性,意味着按照思辨的标准进行检验,这个标准由10个维度构成:清晰性、准确性、精确性、相关性、深刻性、宽广性、逻辑性、完整性、重要性、公正性。一个拥有思辨能力的人具备八大品质，包括：诚实、谦虚、相信理性、坚忍不拔、公正、勇气、同理心、独立思考。

其次，学习者应该掌握具体的思辨方法。如：如何阐释和理解文本信息与观点？如何解析文本结构？如何评价论述的有效性？如何把已有理论和方法运用于新的场景？如何收集和鉴别信息和证据？如何论证说理？如何识别逻辑谬误？如何提问？如何对自己的思维进行反思和矫正？等等等等。

最后，思辨能力的提高必须经过系统的训练。思辨能力的发展是一个从低级思维向高级思维发展的过程，必须运用思辨的标准一以贯之地训练思辨的各要素，在各门课程的学习中练习思辨，在实际工作中使用思辨，在日常生活中体验思辨，最终使良好的思维习惯成为第二本能。

"思想者指南丛书"旨在为教师教授思辨方法、学生学习思辨技能和社会大众提高思辨能力提供最为简明和最为实用的操作指南。该套丛书直接从西方最具影响力的思辨能力研究和培训机构（The Foundation for Critical Thinking）原版引进，共21册，包括"基础篇"：《批判性思维术语手册》、《批判性思维概念与方法手册》、《大脑的奥秘》、《批判性思维与创造性思维》、《什么是批判性思维》、《什么是分析性思维》；"大众篇"：《识别逻辑谬误》、《思维的标准》、《如何提问》、《像苏格拉底一样提问》、《什么是伦理推理》、《什么是工科推理》、《什么是科学思维》；"教学篇"：《透视教育时尚》、《思辨能力评价标准》、《思辨阅读与写作测评》、《如何促进主动学习与合作学习》、《如何提升学生的学习能力》、《如何通过思辨学好一门学科》、《如何进行思辨性阅读》、《如何进行思辨性写作》。

由理查德·保罗和琳达·埃尔德两位思辨能力研究领域的全球顶级大师领衔研发的"思想者指南丛书"，享誉北美乃至全球，销售数百万册，被美国中小学、高等学校乃至公司和政府部门普遍用于教学、培训和人才选拔。该套丛书具有如下特点：其一，语言简洁明快，具有一般英文水平的读者都能阅读；其二，内容生动易懂，运用大量的具体例子解释思辨的理论和方法；其三，针对性和操作性极强，教师可以从"教学篇"子系列中获取指导教学改革的思辨教学策略与方法，学生也可从"教学篇"子系列中找到提高不同学科学习能力的思辨技巧；一般社会人士可以通过"大众篇"子系列掌握思辨的通用技巧，提高在社会场景中分析问题和解决问题的能力；各类读者都可以通过"基础篇"子系列掌握思维的基本规律和思辨的基本理论。

总之，思辨能力的高下将决定一个人学业的优劣、事业的成败乃至一个民族的兴衰。在此意义上，我向全国中小学教师、高等学校教师和学生以及社会大众郑重推荐"思想者指南丛书"。相信该套丛书的普及阅读和学习运用，必将有利于促进教育改革，提高人才培养质量，提升大众思辨能力，为创新型国家建设和社会文明进步作出深远的贡献。

孙有中
2016年春于北京外国语大学

Contents

Daily Emphasis

Introduction

When students think within the content of our courses, they take ownership of the most basic principles and concepts within the subjects we teach. The instructional ideas in this guide are premised in this understanding. Most of our suggestions represent possible teaching strategies. They are based on a vision of instruction implied by critical thinking and an analysis of the weaknesses typically found in most traditional didactic lecture/quiz/test formats of instruction. We begin with two premises:

- that to learn a subject well, students must master the thinking that defines that subject, and

- that we, in turn, as their instructors, must design activities and assignments that require students to think actively within the concepts and principles of the subject.

Students should *master* fundamental concepts and principles before they attempt to learn more advanced concepts. If class time is focused on helping students perform well on these foundational activities, we feel confident that the goals of most instruction will be achieved.

It is up to you, the instructor, to decide which of these ideas you will test in the classroom. Only you can decide how to teach your students. Our goal is not to dictate to you, but to provide you with possible strategies with which to experiment. The specific suggestions we recommend represent methods and strategies we have developed and tested with our students. Judge for yourself their plausibility. Test them for their practicality. Those that work (i.e., improve instruction), keep; those that do not work, abandon or re-design.

The suggestions overlap each other and make most sense when taken together, as an interrelated network. Often one suggestion is made intelligible in the light of two or three others. So if one is not clear to you, read on. The strength of each of them, in re-enforcing each other, will then become increasingly clear.

Recommended Design Features

Idea # 1:

Design instruction so that students engage in routine practice in internalizing and applying the concepts they are learning (and in evaluating their understanding of each).

For students to learn any new concept well they must first internalize the concept, then apply the concept to a problem or issue so that they come to see the value of understanding the concept. At the same time, they need to evaluate how well they are internalizing and applying the concepts they are learning.

If students are to acquire understandings and skills, we need to provide many opportunities for them to

1. internalize the key concepts in the subject, and to

2. apply those concepts to problems and issues (in their lives or in their course-work).

It is only when students apply what they are learning to actual situations or problems that they come to see the value in what they are learning. And only when they see the value in learning the content will they be internally motivated to do so.

At the same time students are internalizing concepts and applying them in a meaningful way, they need practice in evaluating their work. Self-assessment is an integral part of educated thinking; it would be unintelligible to say of a person that he is thinking in an educated manner, but is not skilled in evaluating his thinking. In the same way, it would be unintelligible to say of a student that he is learning a subject well but does not know how to evaluate his learning.

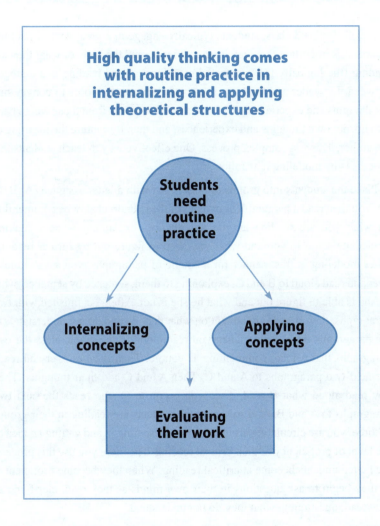

High quality thinking comes with routine practice in internalizing and applying theoretical structures

Students need routine practice

Internalizing concepts

Applying concepts

Evaluating their work

Idea # 2:
Teach students how to assess their reading.

In a well-designed class, students typically engage in a great deal of reading. Hence, it is important that they learn to "figure out" the logic of what they are reading (the logically interconnected meanings). Good reading is a dialogue between the reader and the text. The writer has chosen words to convey his/her thoughts and experiences. The reader must translate from those words back into his/her own thoughts and experiences, and thereby capture the meaning of the author. This is a complex process. One effective way to teach students this process is by modeling it as follows:

Place the students into groups of three, each with a letter assigned (A, B, or C). You then read a paragraph or two out of the text aloud slowly, commenting on what you are reading as you are reading, explaining what is making immediate sense to you and what you need to figure out by further reading. After modeling in this manner for a couple of paragraphs, you ask A to take over and read aloud to B and C, explaining to them, sentence by sentence, what he/she is able to figure out and what he/she is not. After A is finished with two paragraphs, then B and C comment on what they do and do not understand (in the paragraphs that A read). Then you read aloud to the whole class the two paragraphs that A read, commenting as you go. Then B takes over and reads the next two paragraphs to A and C. Then A and C add their thoughts. Then you read aloud what B read. Then you go on to C who reads the next two paragraphs to A and B. And so on. As the students are reading in their groups of three, you are circulating around the room listening in and getting an idea of the level of proficiency of their critical reading. The more you use this process, the better students become at critical reading. When they become proficient at it, they begin to ask questions in their own minds as they read, clarifying as they read, questioning what they do not understand.

See also the thinker's guide to *How to Read a Paragraph* (The Art of Close Reading).

Idea # 3:

Teach students how to assess their writing.

Good thinking is thinking that (effectively) assesses itself. As a critical thinker, I do not simply state the problem; I assess the clarity of my own statement. I do not simply gather information; I check it for its relevance and significance. I do not simply form an interpretation; I check to make sure my interpretation has adequate evidentiary support.

Because of the importance of self-assessment to critical thinking, it is important to bring it into the structural design of the course and not just leave it to random or chance use. Here are a variety of strategies that can be used for fostering self-assessment through peer-assessment:

Assessing Writing

When students are required to bring written papers to class, the activities below can be used as strategies for fostering high quality peer-assessment:

1. **First Strategy**. Working in groups of four, students choose the best paper (using standards of clarity, logic, etc. as well as any other criteria you have given them). Then they join with a second group and choose the best paper of the two (one from each group). These papers (chosen by the 8-person groups) are collected and read to the class as a whole. A class-wide discussion is held, under your direction, to make clear the strengths and weaknesses of the competing remaining papers, leading to the class voting on the best paper of the day (again, always using explicit intellectual standards in the assessment).

2. **Second Strategy**. Working in groups of three or four, students write out their recommendations for improvement on three or four papers (from students not in the group). The written recommendations go back to the original writers who do a revised draft for the next class. Using this method every student receives written feedback on their papers from a "team" of critics.

3. **Third Strategy**. Working in groups of three or four, students take turns reading their papers aloud slowly and discussing the extent to which

they have or have not fulfilled the performance criteria relevant to the paper.

4. **Fourth Strategy**. One student's paper is read aloud slowly to the class while the instructor leads a class-wide discussion on how the paper might be improved. This discussion serves as a model of what is expected in the assessment process. Then the students work in groups of two or three to try to come up with recommendations for improvement for the students in their group (based on the model established by the instructor).

See also the thinker's guide to *How to Write a Paragraph: The Art of Substantive Writing.*

Idea # 4:
Teach students how to assess their speaking.

In a well-designed class, students often engage in oral communication. They articulate what they are learning: explaining, giving examples, posing problems, interpreting information, tracing assumptions, etc… They learn to assess what they are saying, becoming aware of when they are being vague, when they need an example, when their explanations are inadequate, etc… Here are three general strategies you can use to teach students to assess their speaking abilities.

1. **First Strategy**. Students teaching students. One of the best ways to learn is to try to teach someone else. If we have trouble explaining something, it is often because we are not clear about what we are explaining.

2. **Second Strategy**. Group Problem Solving. By putting students in a group and giving them a problem or issue to work on together, their mutual articulation and exchanges will often help them to think better. They often help correct each other, and so learn to "correct" themselves. Make sure that they are routinely applying intellectual standards to their thinking as they discuss issues.

3. **Third Strategy**. Oral test on basic vocabulary. One complex tactic that aids student learning is the oral test. Students are given a vocabulary list. They spend time studying the key concepts for the course. They are then put into groups of twos or threes and are asked to take turns explaining the concepts to each other. They are encouraged to assess each other's explanations. Wander about the class listening in and choose two students who seem prepared for the oral exam. Stop the class and announce that the oral test is going to begin and that you have chosen "X" and "Y" to be tested first. After you test these two students (and they pass), announce to the class that X and Y have passed and that they are now "certified" to test others. However, anyone "certified" by a student tester must be "spot-tested" by you on one item. If any such student fails your spot test, the person who certified them is "de-certified" (and must repeat the exam). Everyone who passes becomes a certifier and gets paired with a student who has not taken the test. By this method, you only test the first two students. For the rest of the process you direct "traffic" and spot-check those

who are "certified" by a peer. During this assessment the tester should be looking for a beginning understanding of the concepts, and the ability to give examples of the concept. Since the students who pass become "certifiers" or "tutors" and are assigned to assess other students (or tutor them), everyone gets multiple experiences explaining, and hearing explanations of, the basic vocabulary. We give a vocabulary list to the students on the first day of class so they know exactly which concepts they will be expected to explain during the oral exam. We give this exam during the first few weeks of the class so students learn the most basic vocabulary early in the course, vocabulary that is then used on a daily basis in class. You might want to modify this exam by giving parts of it during or after each chapter (of the textbook).

Idea # 5:
Teach students how to assess their listening.

Since students spend a good deal of their time listening, and since developing critical listening skills is difficult to achieve, it is imperative that faculty design instruction that fosters critical listening. This is best done by holding students responsible for their "listening" in the classroom. Here are some structures that help students develop critical listening abilities:

1. **First Strategy**. Call on students regularly and unpredictably, holding them responsible either to ask questions they are formulating as they think through the content or to give a summary, elaboration, or example of what others have said.

2. **Second Strategy**. Ask every student to write down the most basic question they need to be answered in order to understand the issue or topic under discussion. Then collect the questions (to see what they understand or don't understand about the topic). Or you might:

    (a) call on some of them to read their questions aloud, or

    (b) put them in groups of two with each person trying to answer the question of the other.

Through activities such as these students learn to monitor their listening, determining when they are and when they are not following what is being said. This should lead to their asking pointed questions. Reward students for asking questions when they do not understand what is being said.

Idea # 6:

Design tests with the improvements of student thinking in mind.

In planning tests, be clear about your purpose. A test in any subject matter should determine the extent to which students are developing useful and important thinking skills with respect to that subject. The best tests are those most reflective of the kinds of intellectual tasks students will perform when they apply the subject matter to professional and personal issues in the various domains of their lives. Since "multiple choice" tests are rarely useful in assessing life situations, they are rarely the best overall test, though they can assess some supplementary understandings at an entry level.

One type of test that does target more realistic skills is an analytic test of the students' ability to take thinking apart and elaborate accurately each of its elements. Another type tests the student's ability to evaluate those elements using intellectual standards. In other words, students should learn how to analyze and evaluate thinking within the subjects they are studying.

Part One. Analyzing Thinking. After students have learned the fundamentals of critical thinking, and have reasoned through the logic of several chapters and/or articles you have given them, you might have them figure out the logic of an article during one class period (or the logic of a section of the textbook). Through this test, you can determine the extent to which they can accurately state an author's purpose, key question, information, conclusions, concepts, assumptions, implications, and point of view.

Part Two. Evaluating Thinking. Having completed Part One above, you might then have students evaluate the author's logic using the following format (included in *The Miniature Guide to Critical Thinking*):

- Is the **question** at issue clear and unbiased? Does the expression of the question do justice to the complexity of the matter at issue?

- Is the writer's **purpose** clear?

- Does the writer cite relevant evidence, experiences, and/or **information** essential to the issue?

- Does the writer clarify key **concepts** when necessary?

- Does the writer show a sensitivity to what he/she is **assuming** or taking for granted? (Insofar as those assumptions might be reasonably questioned)?

- Does the writer develop a definite line of reasoning, explaining well how he/she is arriving at his/her **conclusions**?

- Does the writer show a sensitivity to alternative **points of view** or lines of reasoning? Does he or she consider and respond to objections framed from other points of view?

- Does the writer show a sensitivity to the **implications** and consequences of the position he or she has taken?

In giving this sort of test, we are trying to determine whether students are learning to enter viewpoints that differ from their own. You can give multiple tests using this same format by changing only the written piece to be analyzed (selecting, of course, pieces whose point of view is significantly different from that of most students). Of course, this test does not determine whether a student will actually empathize with opposing views in real life situations (especially when their vested interest is involved).

Idea # 7:

Make the course "work-intensive" for the students, but not for you.

There are two significant mistakes to avoid. The first is designing classes so students can pass them without thinking deeply about the content of the course. The second is designing classes so that you must work harder than the students. Let us consider both these ideas briefly in turn.

In a class that consists mainly of lectures with periodic quizzes and examinations, students can often get a passing grade by "cramming" the night before quizzes and tests. Many students have developed cramming skills to the point that they misleadingly create the appearance of understanding a body of content (when they don't). The problem is that most cramming feeds only the short-term memory. Students adept at it will say things like, "I got an A in Statistics last semester, but don't ask me any questions about it. I've forgotten most of what I learned."

If students are to become disciplined thinkers, they need to do a good deal of active thinking to take ownership of the content they are learning. Teachers often make the mistake of thinking that students learn well only when instructors spend hours "preparing" for class, (e.g., learning information they then tell to students). But learning to think well requires many opportunities for practice in thinking through problems and issues, and in applying concepts in one's thinking to real life experiences. Students can do this only when we design classroom structure so that they are working to understand and apply the fundamentals of the subject. Spoon feeding passive students is a useless activity. Try random sampling grading to reduce the amount of grading you have to do (see Page 22-23).

Idea # 8:

Use engaged lecture.

When lecture is essential, we recommend use of what we call an "engaged lecture" format. During the lecture, routinely stop and ask students to state in their own words their understanding of what you have said. This can be done through a "random card" format wherein you flip through a set of 3 by 5 cards, each containing one student's name, calling on students randomly as their card happens to come up. You keep shuffling the cards to ensure that each new draw is completely random. You call on students in class to state, elaborate, exemplify, and illustrate (in their own words) the most important points in the lecture or in a chapter in the textbook. This strategy involves every student in the class (since any one of them may be called upon at any moment) and ensures that they are actively listening during the discussion.

In addition, randomly call on students to state in their own words comments made by other students. Begin by selecting one student to state her understanding of a concept or principle you introduced. Then randomly select another student to summarize what the first student said. Then ask the first person if the second person accurately represented what she originally said. We recommend that you do this several times during the lecture so students remain engaged in active listening. Model the kinds of questions you welcome.

Idea # 9:

Require an intellectual journal (when it is relevant to your class).

One powerful strategy for teaching students to assess their own thinking and to apply the concepts they are learning in class to what they think is important in their lives is to require them to write journal entries during the course of the semester. Such a journal provides a bridge between the class and the students' daily experience and decision-making. The goal is to help students get examples of what it would be like to apply critical thinking to significant life situations.

Here is a structure you might use for the journal entries:

1. **Situation**. Describe in detail a significant situation you were in or are in at present. This would be a situation that has caused you to have a strong emotional reaction (most likely a negative reaction). Then describe in detail what happened in the situation. Think of situations such as getting angry when caught in a traffic jam, or acting out because your roommate's music is too loud while you are trying to study. Focus on the everyday sorts of relationship problems that cause you to react irrationally.

2. **Response**. Describe your response to the situation. What precisely did you do in the situation?

3. **Analysis**. Analyze your reaction to the situation. In other words, state what was really going on in your thinking and your behavior. Why did you react the way you did? Was your behavior reasonable in the circumstances?

4. **Implications**. What can you learn from your analysis? Is there something you should do differently in the future to avoid a similar reaction in a similar situation? In short, what did you learn from this analysis that will help you in the future?

Orientation (first few days)

Idea # 10:

Give students a thorough orientation to the course.

Students should know from the beginning how a class is going to be taught, how they are going to be assessed, and what they should be striving to achieve. They should know, from the beginning, what they are going to be doing most of the time and what exactly is expected of them in that process. The aim of the course should be carefully spelled out. If you are emphasizing critical thinking, it is helpful to contrast the aim and design with that of standard didactically taught courses. You might begin the course with something like the following introduction:

"This class is going to be different from any class you have taken thus far because the emphasis will be on actively developing your thinking. Everything we do in this class will be designed to help you become better and better at thinking within the subject. You will therefore not be asked to memorize information rotely. Instead, you will be required to internalize information by using it actively in every class and in class assignments. Each day we will be attempting to improve your thinking. Think of learning about thinking (within the field) as you would of learning a sport. To learn to play tennis, you need to first learn the fundamentals of tennis at an elementary level and then practice those fundamentals during every practice session. The same is true of learning to think better within this field. You must be introduced to the fundamentals of sound thinking. Then you must regularly practice those fundamentals. Therefore I will design every class day with the

primary purpose of helping you develop your thinking or reasoning skills. Why is this important? The quality of every decision you make will be directly determined by the quality of your reasoning abilities. In fact the quality of your life in general will be determined by how well you think in general."

Idea # 11:

Develop a syllabus which highlights your expectations for the students.

You may want to consider using—or modifying for use—the following class syllabus. The requirements are based on a two-class-per-week schedule. It is developed with a science class in mind. Modify it to fit your subject.

Introduction to Science
Sample Class Syllabus

The Key Concept of the Course

This course is entirely concerned with the development of scientific thinking. Humans do not naturally think scientifically; our thinking is often unscientific, or pseudo-scientific. Yet, as humans we live with the unrealistic but confident sense that we, in forming our beliefs, have fundamentally figured out the true nature of things, and that we have done this objectively. We naturally believe in our intuitive perceptions about the physical world—however inaccurate. We do not naturally raise to consciousness our assumptions about how the physical world works, the unscientific way we use information, the uncritical way we interpret data. We do not naturally question our concepts and ideas, or the fact that we often reason from an unscientific perspective.

All of this is true, despite the fact that most people take many years of "science" in school. To become a scientific thinker is to reverse this process by learning to take charge of the ideas one has about the physical world. It is to think consciously and deliberately and skillfully about that world. In short, it means training our minds to think scientifically.

A critical approach to learning science certainly entails organizing and internalizing facts, taking command of technical terminology, and coming to understand scientific procedures—but not in isolation. Our goal in this course will be to learn science as a system of integrally connected meanings that are tied to important ideas in other disciplines. Learning key organizing ideas in science should fundamentally transform the way we see the physical world.

We should take these ideas with us throughout our lives and use them to think through the scientific issues we face.

A critical approach to learning science requires us to ponder questions, propose solutions, and think through possible experiments. Yet many texts treat the concept of "the scientific method" in a misleading way. Not all scientists do the same kinds of things—some experiment, others don't, some do field observations, others build models, and so on. For example, chemists, theoretical physicists, zoologists, and paleontologists pursue different types of questions; the nature of these questions will determine the scientific processes they need to use and the thinking they need to do to answer them. Furthermore, scientific thinking is not a matter of following a step-by-step procedure. Rather it is a kind of thinking in which scientists continually move back and forth between questions they ask about the world, observations they make, and in many instances, experiments they devise to test out various hypotheses, guesses, hunches, and models. Following their lead, when we thinking scientifically, we continually think hypothetically: "If this idea of mine is true, then what will happen under these or those conditions? Let me see, suppose we try this. What does this result tell me? Why did this happen? If this is why, then that should happen when I..." It is more important for you to get into the habit of thinking scientifically than to get the correct answer through a rote process you do not understand. The essential point is this: you should do your own thinking about scientific questions from the start. Your role is not to passively take in what scientists or textbooks tell you. Rather it is to grasp the spirit of scientific thinking.

Scientific Thinking Seeks to Quantify, Explain and Predict Relationships in Nature

Scientific thinking is based on a belief in the intelligibility of nature, that is, upon the belief that the same cause operating under the same conditions, will result in the same effects at any time. As a result of this belief, scientists pursue the following goals.

1. **They observe**. (What conditions seem to affect the phenomena we are observing?) In order to determine the causal relations of physical occurrences or phenomena, scientists seek to identify factors that affect what they are studying.

2. **They design experiments**. (When we isolate potential causal factors, which seem to most directly cause the phenomena, and which do not?) In scientific experiments, the experimenter sets up the experiment so as to maintain control over all likely causal factors being examined. Experimenters then isolate each variable and observe its effect on the phenomena being studied to determine which factors are essential to the causal effect.

3. **They strive for exact measurement**. (What are the precise quantitative relationships between essential factors and their effects?) Scientists seek to determine the exact quantitative relationships between essential factors and resulting effects.

4. **They seek to formulate physical laws**. (Can we state the precise quantitative relationship in the form of a law?) The quantitative cause-effect relationship, with its limitations clearly specified, is known as a physical law. For example, it is found that for a constant mass of gas, at a constant temperature, the volume is inversely related to the pressure applied to it; in other words, the greater the pressure the less the volume—the greater the volume the less the pressure. This relationship is constant for most gases within a moderate range of pressure. This relationship is known as Boyle's Law. It is a physical law because it defines a cause-effect relationship, but it does not explain the relationship.

5. **They study related or similar phenomena**. (When we examine many related or similar phenomena, can we make a generalization that covers them all?) A study of many related or similar phenomena is typically carried out to determine whether a generalization or hypothesis can be formulated that accounts for, or explains, them all.

6. **They formulate general hypotheses or physical theories**. A theoretical generalization is formulated (if one is found to be plausible). For example, the kinetic theory of gas was formulated to explain what is documented in Boyle's Law. According to this theory, gases are aggregates of discrete molecules that incessantly fly about and collide with themselves and the wall of the container that holds them. The smaller the space they are forced to occupy, the

greater the number of collisions against the surfaces of the space.

7. **They seek to test, modify, and refine hypotheses**. If a generalization is formulated, scientists test, modify, and refine it through comprehensive study and experimentation, extending it to all known phenomena to which it may have any relation, restricting its use where necessary, or broadening its use in suggesting and predicting new phenomena.

8. **They seek to establish general physical laws as well as comprehensive physical theories**. General physical laws and comprehensive physical theories are broadly applicable in predicting and explaining the physical world. The Law of Gravitation, for example, is a general physical law. It states that every portion of matter attracts every other portion with a force directly proportional to the product of the two masses, and inversely proportional to the square of the distance between the two. Darwin's Theory of Evolution is a comprehensive physical theory. It holds that all species of plants and animals develop from earlier forms by hereditary transmission of slight variations in successive generations and that natural selection determines which forms will survive.

9. **They continually seek revolutionary ways of seeing the physical world that emerge out of their research and theory development**. Skilled scientists are not locked into traditional ways of looking at the physical world. They continually seek to develop scientific theory in light of new information. They don't just assimilate new information into existing theories. Rather, when it makes sense to, they reconstruct prior theories and reevaluate prior facts, a revolutionary process that can take many years and many scientists working on the issues. When this happens, whole networks of theories can shift, changing the very way in which scientists understand and deal with the physical world.

Consider this example:

Until Copernicus (1473-1543), people thought the earth was the center of the universe. This erroneous belief was based on the Ptolemaic system and had prevailed since the 2nd century A.C.E. The Copernican revolution was based on the theory that the earth at once revolved around its axis and around the sun in circular orbit. Though he loved the circular beauty of Copernicus's circular orbits, Johann Kepler (1571-1630) abandoned the circle for an elliptical orbit. He suggested that planets travel in such elliptical orbits with the sun in one focus and that the speed of the planets varies with their distance from the sun. He offered a mathematical calculation for tying planets into a harmonious system. If Kepler was right, his theory would required that Aristotle's physics and astronomy be discarded, which had dominated for more than 1000 years. It was Galileo (1564-1642) who conclusively refuted Aristotle, establishing the principle of inertia, which he applied equally to celestial and terrestrial bodies. This principle showed that force is needed, not to keep a body going (as Aristotle had argued) but to stop it or deflect it from its course. Thus Galileo freed science from the qualitative thinking of Aristotle and prepared the way for Newton's work. Galileo's principles and discoveries were fused into one integrated system by Isaac Newton. Newton's three laws of motion dominated the world of physics until Einstein.

The General Plan for the Course

The class will focus on practice not on lecture. It will emphasize your figuring out things about the physical world using your own mind, not memorizing what is in a textbook. On a typical class day you will be in small groups practicing "disciplined scientific" thinking. You will be regularly responsible for assessing your own work using criteria and standards discussed in class. If at any time in the semester you feel unsure about your "grade," you should request an assessment from the instructor.

For every class day you will read sections of the textbook. You will also have a written assignment which involves "disciplined scientific" thinking (most of which will be taken directly from the text).

Whenever you are doing a task in or for the class, ask yourself, would an independent observer closely watching you conclude that you were engaged in "taking charge of your mind, of your ideas about the physical world, of your thinking about that world." Or would such a person conclude that you were "merely going through the motions of doing an assignment," trying to succeed by rote memorization?

Requirements

You must complete all of the following:

1. 27 short written assignments, one due for every class day. Each of these must be typed—so that you can easily revise them. If your assignment for the day is not completed you are not prepared to do the "in-class" work of the day and will be asked to leave.

2. An oral exam. This is a mastery exam involving the basic vocabulary of science. All entries must be passed to pass the exam.

3. A final exam.

4. A Self-Evaluation, in which you "make a case" for receiving a particular grade using criteria provided in class and citing evidence from your work across the semester.

5. Consistent classroom attendance and active, skilled participation.

Grading

The class will not be graded on a curve. It is theoretically possible for the whole class to get an A or an F. You will not be competing against each other and there will be every incentive to help each other improve. No letter grades will be given before the final grade—unless you make a specific request to the professor. You should focus on improving your performance as a scientific thinker, increasing your strengths and diminishing your weaknesses, not in looking for a grade.

- Final Exam: about 20%

- Out of class writing: about 30%

- Self-evaluation: about 25%

- Active, Skilled Participation: about 10%

- Journal: about 15%

- Penalty for Missed Classes: You may miss two classes without receiving any formal penalty (though it is clearly in your interest to attend every class and participate actively). Every two unexcused absences after the first two results in a 1/3 of a grade penalty (Hence, with four absences: if your final grade would have been C+, it would be reduced to a C; if C- it would be reduced to D+). Attendance is taken by way of "stamped in" class assignments.

Since the final grade is not based on points and is not mathematically calculated, the above percentages are approximations to suggest emphasis, not precise figures. In assigning your final grade the instructor will lay all of your work out and match your work as a whole against the criteria passed out in class. You should read and re-read these criteria many times through-out the semester to ensure that you are clear about what you are striving to achieve.

Grading Policies

If you are to develop as a scientific thinker, you will need to develop as a scientific writer as well. And to develop as a writer, you must impose upon yourself the same standards that good writers impose upon themselves. The key question I will ask myself as I grade your written work is "What specifically does your writing demonstrate about your ability to reason scientifically?"

As you write, here are some key points you should keep in mind:

- When you write sentences that can be interpreted in many different ways (and you do not make clear which meaning you intend), you demonstrate that you are writing, and presumably, thinking in a vague way. You should therefore strive to write so that you make clear precisely what you mean. Scientific thinking must be clear and precise.

- When you give concrete examples and illustrations to make your point clear, you demonstrate that you know how to clarify your thought. You should therefore give scientific examples and illustrations wherever clarification of your meaning is needed.

- When you make clear—with appropriate transitional words and critical vocabulary—the logical relations between the sentences you write, you make evident that you are thinking in terms of the logic of scientific thought and that you understand the structure of your own reasoning. You should therefore make clear the logical relations between the sentences and paragraphs you write.

- When you analyze key scientific concepts and demonstrate how to lay bare the logic of them, you make evident that you are skilled at conceptual analysis. You should therefore analyze key scientific concepts in your written work wherever it is needed.

- When you make clear the scientific question or issue you are dealing with and you stick to that issue, you show that you have the intellectual discipline and focus to appreciate what each issue you raise requires of you. You demonstrate that you appreciate the importance of relevance. You should therefore clarify the scientific question you are focused on and stick to that question throughout the written piece, showing how each point is relevant to that question.

- When you make only those assertions that you have sufficiently analyzed empathetically, you demonstrate intellectual humility. You should show in your writing that you have fully considered all reasonable ways of looking at the issue. Scientific thinking does not jump to conclusions.

The Weighting of Papers in the Portfolio

The semester will be divided into thirds. At the end of the course, to determine your grade on the portfolio, I will grade one paper randomly chosen from the first third, two from the second third, and three from the final third. At any point in the course you may turn in your portfolio for grade-level assessment. However, if you are routinely assessing your own work—as scientific thinking requires—you should be able to recognize the level at which you are performing.

Idea # 12:
Give students grade profiles.

What Each Grade Represents

These grade profiles define outlines for grades of A, B, C, D and F. They are suggestive of common denominator academic values and can be contextualized at two levels: the department level (to capture domain-specific variations) and at the course level (to capture course-specific differences.)

The Grade of A

(The essence of A-level work. Excellence overall, no major weaknesses). A-level work implies excellence in thinking and performance within the domain of a subject and course. It also implies development of a range of knowledge acquired through critical thought. The work at the end of the course is, on the whole, clear, precise, and well-reasoned, though with occasional lapses into weak reasoning. In A-level work, terms and distinctions are used effectively. The work demonstrates a mind beginning to take charge of its own ideas, assumptions, inferences, and intellectual processes. The A-level student usually analyzes issues clearly and precisely, usually formulates information clearly, usually distinguishes the relevant from the irrelevant, usually recognizes key questionable assumptions, usually clarifies key concepts effectively, typically uses language in keeping with educated usage, frequently identifies relevant competing points of view, and shows a general tendency to reason carefully from clearly stated premises, as well as noticeable sensitivity to important implications and consequences. A-level work displays excellent reasoning and problem-solving skills. The A student's work is consistently at a high level of intellectual excellence.

The Grade of B

(The essence of B-level work is that it demonstrates more strengths than weaknesses and is more consistent in high level performance than C-level work. It has some distinctive weaknesses, though no major ones). The grade of B implies sound thinking and performance within the domain of a subject and

course. It also implies development of a range of knowledge acquired through critical thought, though this range is not as high as A-level work. B-level work at the end of the course is, on the whole, clear, precise, and well-reasoned, though with occasional lapses into weak reasoning. On the whole, terms and distinctions are used effectively. The work demonstrates a mind beginning to take charge of its own ideas, assumptions, inferences, and intellectual processes. The student often analyzes issues clearly and precisely, often formulates information clearly, usually distinguishes the relevant from the irrelevant, often recognizes key questionable assumptions, usually clarifies key concepts effectively, typically uses language in keeping with educated usage, frequently identifies relevant competing points of view. It shows a general tendency to reason carefully from clearly stated premises, as well as noticeable sensitivity to important implications and consequences. B-level work displays good reasoning and problem-solving skills.

The Grade of C

(The essence of C-level work is that it demonstrates more than a minimal level of skill, but it is also highly inconsistent, with as many weaknesses as strengths). The grade of C implies mixed thinking and performance within the domain of a subject and course. It also implies some development of knowledge acquired through critical thought. Thus C-level work at the end of the course shows some emerging thinking skills within the subject, but also pronounced weaknesses. Though some assignments are reasonably well done, others are poorly done; or at best are mediocre. There are more than occasional lapses in reasoning. Though terms and distinctions are sometimes used effectively, sometimes they are used quite ineffectively. Only on occasion does C-level work display a mind taking charge of its own ideas, assumptions, inferences, and intellectual processes. Only occasionally does C-level work display intellectual discipline and clarity. The C-level student only occasionally analyzes issues clearly and precisely, formulates information clearly, distinguishes the relevant from the irrelevant, recognizes key questionable assumptions, clarifies key concepts effectively, uses language in keeping with educated usage, identifies relevant competing points of view, reasons carefully from clearly stated premises, or recognizes important implications and consequences. Sometimes the C-level student seems to be simply going through the motions of the assignment, carrying out the form without getting into the

spirit of it. On the whole, C-level work shows only modest and inconsistent reasoning and problem-solving skills and sometimes displays weak reasoning and problem-solving skills.

The Grade of D

(The essence of D-Level work is that it demonstrates only a minimal level of understanding and skill in the subject). The grade of D implies poor thinking and performance within the domain of a subject and course. On the whole, the student tries to get through the course by means of rote recall, attempting to acquire knowledge by memorization rather than through comprehension and understanding. On the whole, the student is not developing the skills of thought and knowledge requisite to understanding course content. Most assignments are poorly done. There is little evidence that the student is critically reasoning through assignments. Often the student seems to be merely going through the motions of the assignment, carrying out the form without getting into the spirit of it. D work rarely shows any effort to take charge of ideas, assumptions, inferences, and intellectual processes. In general, D-level thinking lacks discipline and clarity. In D-level work, the student rarely analyzes issues clearly and precisely, almost never formulates information clearly, rarely distinguishes the relevant from the irrelevant, rarely recognizes key questionable assumptions, almost never clarifies key concepts effectively, frequently fails to use language in keeping with educated usage, only rarely identifies relevant competing points of view, and almost never reasons carefully from clearly stated premises, or recognizes important implications and consequences. D-level work does not show good reasoning and problem-solving skills and frequently displays poor reasoning and problem-solving skills.

The Grade of F

(The essence of F-level work is that the student demonstrates a pattern of unskilled thinking and/or fails to do the required work of the course). The student tries to get through the course by means of rote recall, attempting to acquire knowledge by memorization rather than through comprehension and understanding. The student is not developing the skills of thought and knowledge requisite to understanding course content. Here are typical characteristics of the work of a student who receives an F. A close examination reveals: The student does

not understand the basic nature of what it means to think within the subject or discipline, and in any case does not display the thinking skills and abilities which are at the heart of the course. The work at the end of the course is vague, imprecise, and unreasoned as it was in the beginning. There is little evidence that the student is genuinely engaged in the task of taking charge of his/her thinking. Many assignments appear to have been done pro forma, the student simply going through the motions without really putting any significant effort into thinking his/her way through them. Consequently, the student is not analyzing issues clearly, not formulating information clearly, not accurately distinguishing the relevant from the irrelevant, not identifying key questionable assumptions, not clarifying key concepts, not identifying relevant competing points of view, not reasoning carefully from clearly stated premises, or tracing implications and consequences. The student's work does not display discernible reasoning and problem-solving skills.

Idea # 13:
Use a "student understandings" form.

It is important that students clearly understand what instructors expected of them. We therefore recommend the use of a "student understandings" form. This form should be given to students during the orientation to the course, with an explanation of each item. Students then initial each item as you explain it, indicating their understanding. Here are sample items one might include in such a form:

Student Understandings

1. I understand that there are intellectual standards in this course and that I am responsible for monitoring my own learning._____

2. I understand that the class will focus on practice not on lecture._____

3. I understand that on a typical class day I will be working in a small group and that I will be responsible to take an active part in advancing the assigned work of the group._____

4. I understand that I will be held regularly responsible for assessing my own work using criteria and standards discussed in class._____

5. I understand that if at any time in the semester I feel unsure about my "grade," I may request an assessment from the instructor(s)._____

6. I understand that I must keep a journal, using a special format and including 20 entries in the course of the semester._____

7. I understand that there are 27 short written assignments, one due for several class days._____

8. I understand that if an assignment is due for a class day and it is not completed, then I am not prepared to do the "in-class" work of the day and will be asked to leave. I understand that I may return to class once the assignment is completed._____

9. I understand that there is an oral exam that is a mastery exam. I understand that all entries must be passed to pass the course._____

10. I understand that there is a final exam in the course._____

11. I understand that I must do A Self-Evaluation, in which I "make a case" for

receiving a particular grade using criteria provided in class and citing evidence from my work across the semester._____

12. I understand that the work of the course requires <u>consistent classroom attendance</u> and active participation._____

13. I understand that the class will not be graded on a curve. I understand that it is theoretically possible for the whole class to get an A or an F._____

14. I understand the basis of the final grade as outlined in the syllabus._____

15. I understand that since the final grade is not based on points and is not mathematically calculated; the percentages outlined in the syllabus are approximations to suggest emphasis, not precise figures. In assigning my final grade the professor will lay all of my work out before her and match my work as a whole against criteria passed out in class and using the weighting above.

NAME *(print and sign)* _____

Idea # 14:

Explain to the students, when orienting them to the class, what will happen on a typical class day (and why).

In planning what happens on a daily basis in class, we suggest you develop a routine that directly involves students in thinking. What most students are used to doing is sitting back passively and listening impressionistically to a lecture, taking some notes as the spirit moves them. This is usually an ineffective way to internalize class content. In most classes students need practice in active listening, active reading and writing, and disciplined discussion. Designing a typical class day so that students are required (by the design) to be actively and thoughtfully involved is important.

Here is a possible format you might want to use in creating your "typical day":

1. At the end of each class period, assign some section from the textbook for students to read.

2. Where possible, ask students to write out their answers to key questions within those sections.

3. When students come to class on the next class day, place them in pairs or triads.

4. Have each student read his/her paper aloud to the group.

5. As the student is reading his/her paper aloud, have the other students in the group give the reader feedback on his/her paper, focusing on two or three intellectual standards such as clarity, relevance, depth.

6. Then lead a brief discussion of the chapter or section you are focused on, using an engaged lecture format or Socratic dialogue.

7. At the end of the class period, assign another section for the students to read and on the next class day begin this process again.

Idea # 15:

Explain the key concepts of the course explicitly during the first couple of class meetings.

It is helpful to students if from the outset of the course they are clear about the key or "organizing idea" of the course. This is the foundational or guiding concept underlying everything you will be teaching in a given course. We suggest that you use as the organizing idea the mode of thinking that underlies the course. For example, the key idea behind most history courses should be "historical thinking." For most biology courses: "biological thinking." For most nursing courses: "thinking like a professional nurse." To help students understand the guiding idea for the course, discuss the logic of it with them. For example, "The purpose of scientific thinking is …," "The kinds of questions chemists raise are…," "The kind of information they collect is…," and so forth. Give examples of the thinking in action and give the students an activity in which they can experience doing the thinking in an elementary way.

If the course is interdisciplinary or deals with a range of modes of thinking (as, say, many English classes are), then we suggest that you choose as your guiding idea: "thinking critically about X, Y, and Z." For example, "We will focus in this class on thinking critically in reading and writing, and with respect to novels, poems, and plays."

Idea # 16:

Discuss class time as a time in which the students will PRACTICE thinking (within the content) using the fundamental concepts and principles of the field.

When teaching historical thinking, biological thinking, mathematical thinking, sociological thinking, anthropological thinking, thinking like an engineer, thinking like a professional nurse, thinking like an effective student, etc.

1. Approach every class session with a clear sense of the relevant thinking you are looking for in the students.

2. Be prepared to model or dramatize (in front of the students) the thinking you want.

3. Design activities so that students both generate and assess thinking

In other words, in teaching for critical thinking in a subject, you should design the class so that you model the thinking you are looking for. This requires you either to think aloud in front of the class or to present the class with thinking in written form. Once modeled for the students, we should look for the students to engage in practice that emulates the model (not slavishly but in the spirit of the model of course). Shortly after the students engage in some guided practice, they need to assess that practice, discovering thereby their strengths and weaknesses— their present level of understanding. This discovery should become a daily part of their learning, not something they discover six weeks down the line after receiving the results of a quiz.

Encourage students in the thinking you want

Model the thinking you want

Hold students responsible for the thinking they do

Idea # 17:

Make the point that the content is a SYSTEM of interconnected ideas.

Explain that this system is used, by professionals, to ask questions, gather data or information, make inferences about the data, trace implications, and transform the way we see and think about the dimension of the world that the subject represents. For example, the following ideas are part of a system that defines modern chemistry: matter, physical properties, chemical properties, atoms, compounds molecules, the periodic table, law of conservation of mass, atomic and molecular weights, mass number, atomic number, isotopes, ions, etc... Each idea is explained in terms of other ideas. The ideas together form an interrelated system. Model the system of ideas in the content you are teaching by thinking aloud slowly and deliberately before the students. Explain what you are doing and how you are doing it. Proceed in such a way that the students can replicate your example.

Idea # 18:
Think of yourself as a coach.

Think of your students as players being coached. One of the most important qualities of the critical thinking teacher is the ability to "coach" students in thinking, to become *facilitators of learning* rather than "givers of information." Make sure that in class the students are performing for you and that you are not performing for them (while they sit back like spectators at a ball game). The students should see the class principally as a place for **active engagement in a disciplined performance**. We in turn should be there on the sidelines coaching them, making sure they are performing as they should. We should be ready, as it were, to blow the whistle when we see the class failing to "perform" the assigned tasks in the right way or in the right spirit. We should design the class so that it is difficult for the students to adopt a passive role.

We therefore recommend that you spend the majority of your time coaching students on the sidelines, listening to peer interaction, providing feedback on the sorts of problems *in thinking* they are engaged in. In other words, just as in teaching basketball you would focus on coaching players to play basketball better, in teaching content that requires thinking you want to coach students *to think better within that content*. If basketball players are to learn to play better basketball they must learn the fundamentals of basketball and then get on the court and practice playing the game while focusing on the fundamentals. And they must do this over and over again. In the same way, if students are to learn to think within a content field, they must learn the fundamentals of good thinking and then practice thinking through problems and issues within the content. They must do this over and over again, hundreds of times.

This role of "coaching" rather than "imparting information" is very challenging. It is easy to fall into the "cover the content" trap. But we must ask ourselves whether we are covering the content or whether *the students* are covering it. You can cover lots and lots of content in a one-semester course. That is, you can "give" lots of information to students. But that doesn't mean that your students are able to *use* it in any meaningful way. If students are to learn anything well they must actively bring what they are learning into the structures of their minds. They do this through reading, writing, speaking, thinking and rethinking the ideas into their thinking.

Idea # 19:

Discuss the textbook
as the thinking of the author.

Explain to the students that all the content in the textbook is a product of the thinking of the author and that to learn that content, it must be re-constructed in their thinking. Thus in reading chapter one, students should actively "think" the ideas within it, forming the connections in their minds that the text itself is making. The words of the text provide the means by which they enter into and experience the thinking of the subject. To write a history text, the author must think historically. To write a biology text, the author must think biologically. To read both, the student must first think historically and then think biologically. A close reading of the text should provide the students the means—that is, if they have learned the art of close reading.

To see this process with examples, read the guide, *How to Read a Paragraph* (The Art of Close Reading).

Daily Emphasis

Idea # 20:

Encourage students to think — quite explicitly — about their thinking.

Give them specific suggestions for how to go about it. For example, most students left to themselves do not think very effectively as learners. Many have poor reading and listening habits. Most rarely ask questions. Most could not explain the thinking they are using in the learning process. Much of their thinking turns out to be short-term memorization (rote learning). We suggest that you discuss with students the kind of thinking they need to do to master the content you are teaching.

You should point out to students the danger of relying on rote memorization and periodic cramming as a way to try to pass the course. You should tell the students on the first class day that thinking through the content is the key agenda in the course and that this task will be the business of the class.

Idea # 21:

Encourage students to think of content as a form of thinking.

For example, encourage students to recognize that the key to history (as a body of content) is historical thinking, and that the key to biology is biological thinking, etc... Discuss the purposes that define the field of study — "Biologists have the following aims: ...". Name and explain some of the kinds of questions, problems, and issues that people in the field answer, solve, or resolve. Give examples of the way in which data is collected in the field and of the way those data are processed (the inferences or conclusions that professionals come to). Discuss the point of view or perspective that the field involves. How do biologists look at the world (or at the data they collect)? How do anthropologists? How do artists? Nurses? Lawyers? Doctors?

There is a particular set of performances we are striving for in teaching any body of content. We want basic concepts to be internalized. We want students to leave our classes with the content of the course available to them in their minds, so that they can actually use the content they learned in the "real" world. Thinking is the only vehicle for that internalization and use. When students think poorly while learning, they learn poorly. When they think well while learning, they learn well.

Idea # 22:

Relate content whenever possible to issues, problems, and practical situations in the lives of the students.

Students (like all of us) spend most of their time thinking about what they personally value. Their emotional life keeps them focused on the extent to which they are "successfully" achieving their personal values—as measured by their personal thinking. We shall be successful in helping our students begin to think critically only insofar as we are able to stimulate students to grasp the relevance of skilled thinking to their personal life. If a student is personally to value skilled thinking—and hence to strive to practice it unmotivated by a class or a grade—that student must discover the relevance of that thinking to his own life. When we relate historical thinking, for example, to the historical thinking that students unknowingly do in their everyday life, we lay the foundation for their valuing mastery of historical thinking.

Idea # 23:

Target common student disabilities using specific strategies that take them into account.

In an ideal world, students would come to us as self-initiating, skilled learners. If they did, we could easily help them acquire an education. In fact, if students came to school as self-initiating, skilled learners, they would not need official classes at all. They would only need a good library and some advice on how best to study and learn. They would impose assignments on themselves and do the work required to master the subjects they were individually studying. When they acquired, or felt they had acquired, the required level of knowledge in a subject, they could then be tested and certified (or re-directed) accordingly.

Unfortunately, most students arrive with a relatively low level of motivation to learn. What is more, they have few of the skills essential to the process of learning. Most have a predictable set of deficiencies that it does well to recognize from the outset so that one can take them into account in the design and conduct of instruction. In our experience, the following characterizations profile the weaknesses of the overwhelming majority of students. In general, students:

- do only what they are required to do
- tend to put off work on a project until they have a pressing deadline
- are weak listeners
- are weak readers
- are weak writers
- are weak oral communicators
- do not use language with care and precision
- have no intellectual standards
- do not know how to assess:
  — their own work
  — their own thinking
  — their own emotions
  — their own life

Each of these characteristics, when present, requires instructional strategies

41

that "correct" for them. For example, if students **do only what they are required to do and put off work on projects until they have a pressing deadline**, then we have little choice but to design instruction so that there are frequent requirements. Many shorter assignments force students to do more regular work and hence produce a higher quality of learning than a few long assignments. In line with this thinking, we usually assign a short paper for every class day. We treat this paper as a "ticket" to class (those who do not have it done are asked to go to the library and complete it). We use random-sampling grading to avoid having to "grade" anything but a small sampling of the papers assigned, while yet designing day-to-day work so that students get immediate feedback (by participating in self-assessment groups).

Idea # 24:

Use tactics that encourage active learning.

Use the following tactics during class to ensure that students are actively engaged in thinking about the content. They should be routinely called upon to:

1. Summarize in their own words what the teacher or a student has said.

2. Elaborate on what has been said.

3. Relate the issue or content to their own knowledge and experience.

4. Give examples to clarify or support what they have said.

5. Make connections between related concepts.

6. Restate the instructions or assignment in their own words.

7. State the question at issue.

8. Describe to what extent their point of view on the issue is different from or similar to the point of view of the instructor, other students, the author, etc.

9. Take a few minutes to put the above responses into written form.

10. Write down the most pressing question on their mind at this point. The instructor then uses the above tactics to help students reason through the questions.

11. Discuss any of the above with a partner and then participate in a group discussion facilitated by the instructor.

Idea # 25:

Routinely ask questions that probe student understanding of the content.

Questions such as:

1. **Focusing on purpose**: What is the purpose of this chapter? What is the principal function of this system?

2. **Focusing on question**: What questions are emerging for you as we think our way through this issue? What is the key question in this chapter? What is the key question in this section of the chapter?

3. **Focusing on information**: What information did the authors use in coming to these conclusions? How can we check to see if this information is accurate?

4. **Focusing on inference**: What can we logically conclude based on the information presented in this chapter? What conclusions did the authors come to? Were these conclusions justified given the evidence? Is there a more reasonable interpretation of the evidence than the conclusions these "experts" have come to?

5. **Focusing on assumptions**: What do these authors take for granted in reasoning through this issue? Should we accept these assumptions or question them?

6. **Focusing on concepts**: What are the key concepts presented in the chapter (or in the textbook as a whole)? How would you elaborate your understanding of the concepts we have been discussing?

7. **Focusing on implications**: If the authors are correct in the way they conceptualize critical thinking, what are some implications for your life if you learn to think critically? And if you don't?

8. **Focusing on point-of-view**: What are the authors focused upon in this chapter, and how are they seeing it?

Calling on students needs not be intimidating. It can be done in a "non-threatening" fashion. Students then come to accept it as part of the process of learning. We have found no better strategy for teaching critical listening. When we introduce students to this method, we remind them that we are concerned with the development of their thinking, and that we are not using this approach to intimidate them or make them appear ignorant in front of their friends. We then explain the purpose of the process—which is of course to help them improve their critical listening abilities, to be more effective listeners.

Idea # 26:

Model skilled thinking
for your students.

It is most likely the case that your students are unaware of what highly skilled thinking looks like. They have probably rarely seen it modeled, and even then it was probably only implicitly modeled. Rather than just thinking well in front of students, we advocate **explicit modeling** of skilled "moves." This means not only thinking aloud in front of students, but also calling attention to the "moves" you are making.

Examples: In modeling disciplined thinking you might make moves such as these:

- *Focusing on purpose and question* "If I had to solve a problem like this, I would first make clear what my main purpose is as well as the precise question I am trying to solve. So let's take a couple of minutes to do that…"

- *Focusing on implications* "Whenever I am thinking through an important complicated decision, I always want to think through the implications of the various decisions I might come to. In other words, I want to figure out what the likely consequences would be if I reasoned to this decision or that decision."

- *Focusing on concepts* "I realize that it is important to understand how authors are using concepts in their thinking. I therefore want to clarify the key concepts in the articles and books that I read. Let's think aloud about what the author means when she uses the concept of x. I'll begin. Perhaps she means y. Is that an accurate interpretation?"

- *Focusing on clarity* "I always want to be clear about the issue I am dealing with, about what another person is saying, about what I am reading, etc. Therefore when I am unclear in a discussion, I ask questions of clarification. When I am unclear about the issue at hand, I focus on clarifying the question — either by re-expressing the question in my own mind or by asking others to clarify it. As I am reading, I repeat in my mind my understanding of the author's meaning. I figure out what I understand and what I don't understand about what the author is saying."

- *Focusing on accuracy* "Whenever I am reasoning through a problem, I want to make sure I am using accurate information. Whenever it seems that other people are using questionable information in their thinking, I want to check to see if the information is accurate rather than simply accept it as true. I might ask the person how they know the information they are using is accurate. Or I might just look up the information for myself — depending on the circumstances."

- *Focusing on relevance and precision* "Whenever I am reasoning through a problem, I want to make sure I use information relevant to the problem. I do this by writing out the question at issue as precisely as possible and then writing down the information I am using in thinking through the problem. In this way I can check to make sure the information is relevant to the precise question I am dealing with."

- *Focusing on breadth* "In reasoning through this issue it seems that it is important that I consider multiple ways of looking at the issue. I know this because whenever I am dealing with a problem that can reasonably be viewed from multiple relevant viewpoints I want to make sure I fully consider those viewpoints. If I fail to do so I will be reasoning in a narrow-minded way. So let me begin by stating the basic arguments that can reasonably be made with respect to this issue. Then you can see whether I have left out an important perspective."

For other intellectual moves you intend to model for students, refer to the questions that derive from the elements of reasoning and the intellectual standards (see suggestions below).

In modeling the thinking you want students to learn, you should point out exactly what intellectual moves you are making, why you are making them and invite students to critique the moves you are making. One strategy for doing this is to have the students observe the questions you are asking and the thinking you are displaying and then discuss the moves you made. In any case, you want to make it clear that your primary intention is to help students learn to use these "moves" in their thinking while learning and applying the content of the course.

Idea # 27:
Cultivate important intellectual traits in instruction.

You should look for opportunities to model intellectual perseverance, intellectual autonomy, intellectual courage, etc. Consider intellectual humility, for example. Students cannot develop as thinkers if they are not willing to critique their thinking and behavior. Unfortunately, through traditional schooling, students are not taught how to identify flaws in their thinking. Rather they are implicitly taught to cover up their weaknesses, to hide them. They are sometimes told that it is OK to make mistakes, but they quickly learn the negative consequences that come from making mistakes and admitting that there are problems in their thinking. Intellectual humility is rarely modeled for them. For example, they rarely hear teachers discussing the limitations of their own knowledge. They rarely, for example, hear teachers say such things as:

"I don't know the answer to that, but let's think through this problem together, realizing that we don't perhaps have all the relevant information we would need to solve the problem." Or, "yesterday I was asked a question to which I answered x, but upon reflection I realized that I answered superficially. There are complexities I should have mentioned. I became a victim of what is a common problem with thinking. We often go with our immediate response rather than taking time to think something through."

Our purpose in "thinking aloud" is, in this context, to demonstrate how intellectual humility might be manifested in everyday exchanges. We want to show students that skilled thinkers readily admit the limits of their knowledge, ask questions when they are unclear, and change their thinking when they hear arguments more reasonable than their own. In short, we want to demonstrate the need for intellectual humility and the danger of intellectual arrogance. Students learn best those things we exemplify for them.

Idea # 28:

Bring intellectual standards into daily use.

Intellectual standards are essential to the assessment of thinking. Most students cannot name a single standard they use to assess thinking. It is therefore important to bring intellectual standards into daily classroom activities. One way to move in this direction is to routinely ask students questions that require them to apply intellectual standards to their thinking:

- I'm not clear about your position. Could you state it in other words? (**clarity**)

- Could you be more precise? (**precision**)

- How can we check to see if the information you are using is accurate? (**accuracy**)

- How is what you are saying relevant to the question on the floor? (**relevance**)

- Can you articulate how you have considered the complexities in the issue? (**depth**)

- Can you articulate other reasonable ways of looking at the issue? (**breadth**)

- Is there a more logical interpretation than the one you have articulated? (**logic**)

- Have you focused on the most significant issue in dealing with this problem? (**significance**)

Idea # 29:

Have students role play ideas other than their own.

Students are often quick to judge and criticize the thinking of others before they fully understand it. One way to combat this tendency is to help students learn to reason within the point of others (before critiquing the views of others). Here is one way to do this:

1. Give students an article or a section of the textbook to read. Ask them to complete the logic of it (see Idea # 15, and the example below).

2. When students come to class, having figured out to the best of their ability the logic of the article or section, place them in groups of two. One student assumes the role of the "author" of the written piece. The other student questions the "author."

3. Give the following directions to the "author."

   "Imagine yourself as the author of this article. In other words, try your best to think within her/his logic. Articulate to your partner your reasoning, including your purpose in writing the article, the main issue and the key question you are concerned with in the article, the information you used in reasoning through the fundamental issue, the main conclusions you came to, the assumptions you began with (i.e., whatever you took for granted as you wrote the article), the primary concepts you used in reasoning, and the implications which follow if your reasoning is sound.

   Try to think through and articulate how the author might answer any objections to her/his line of reasoning in the most insightful way.

Your partner will question you during the process, primarily focusing on clarifying and assessing the accuracy of what you are saying, and to probe for depth of understanding."

Idea # 30:
Systematically question students using a Socratic approach.

The oldest, and still the most powerful, teaching tactic for fostering excellent thinking is Socratic teaching. In Socratic teaching we focus on asking students questions, not giving them answers. We model an inquiring, probing mind by frequently asking probing questions. Fortunately, the abilities we gain by focusing on the elements of reasoning, prepare us for Socratic questioning. Remember, there is a predictable set of relationships that hold for all subjects and disciplines, since every subject has been developed by those who had:

- shared **goals** and objectives (which defined the subject focus),
- shared **questions** and problems (whose solution they pursued),
- shared **information** and data (which they used as an empirical basis),
- shared modes of **interpreting** or judging that information,
- shared specialized **concepts** and ideas (which they used to help them organize their data),
- shared key **assumptions** (that gave them a basis from which to collectively begin), and
- a shared **point-of-view** (which enabled them to pursue common goals from a common framework).

Each of the elements represents a dimension to be questioned. We can question goals and purposes. We can probe into the nature of the question, problem, or issue that is on the floor. We can inquire into whether or not we have relevant data and information. We can consider alternative interpretations of the data and information. We can analyze key concepts and ideas. We can question assumptions being made. We can ask students to trace out the implications and consequences of what they are saying. We can consider alternative points of view. All of these, and more, are the proper focus of the Socratic questioner.

As a tactic and approach, Socratic questioning is a highly disciplined process. The Socratic questioner acts as the logical equivalent of the inner disciplined voice of reason (which the mind develops when it develops excellent thinking in any subject). The contributions from the members of the class are like so many thoughts in the mind. All of the thoughts must be dealt with and they must be dealt with carefully and fairly. By following up all student answers with further questions, and by selecting questions which advance the discussion, the Socratic questioner forces the class to think in a disciplined, intellectually responsible manner, by continually aiding the students by facilitating questions.

A Socratic questioner should: a) keep the discussion focused, b) keep the discussion intellectually responsible, c) stimulate the discussion with probing questions, d) periodically summarize what has and what has not been dealt with and/or resolved, and e) draw as many students as possible into the discussion.

Epilogue:

Summarize the ideas above in brief to make the whole more intelligible.

Here is a sample of the many ideas summarized in this guide:

1. Let students know what they're in for. On the first day of class, spell out as completely as possible what your philosophy of education is, how you are going to structure the class and why, why the students will be required to think their way through it, why standard methods of rote memorization will not work, what strategies you have in store for them to combat the strategies they use for passing classes without much thinking, etc.

2. Design coverage so that students grasp the fundamental ideas intrinsic to the content. Plan instruction so students attain organizing concepts that enable them to retain more of what you teach. Cover less when more entails that they learn less.

3. Spell out explicitly the intellectual standards you will be using in your grading, and why. Teach the students, as well as you can, how to assess their own work using those standards.

4. Focus on fundamental and powerful concepts with high generalizability. Don't cover more than 50 basic concepts in any one course. Spend the time usually spent introducing more concepts applying and analyzing the basic ones while engaged in problem-solving and reasoned application.

5. Present concepts, as far as possible, in the context of their use as functional tools for the solution of real problems and the analysis of significant issues.

6. Keep the logic of the most basic concepts in the foreground, continually re-weaving new concepts into the basic ones. Talk about the whole in relation to the parts and the parts in relation to the whole.

7. In general design all activities and assignments, including readings, so that students must think their way through them. Lead discussions on the kind of thinking that is required.

8. Develop specific strategies for cultivating critical reading, writing, speaking, and listening. Assume that your students enter your class—as indeed they do—with limited skills in these essential learning modalities.

9. Call frequently on students who don't have their hands up. Then, when one student says something, call on other students to summarize in their own words what the first student said (so that they actively listen to each other).

10. Break the class frequently down into small groups (of twos, threes, fours, etc.), give the groups specific tasks and specific time limits, and call on particular groups afterward to report back on what part of their task they completed, what problems occurred, how they tackled those problems, etc.

11. Require regular writing for class. But grade using random sampling to make it possible for you to grade student writing without having to read it all (which you probably won't have time for).

12. Speak less so that they think more.

13. Don't be a mother robin — chewing up the text for the students and putting it into their beaks through lecture. Teach them instead how to read the text for themselves, actively and analytically. Focus, in other words, on teaching students how to read the text not on "reading the text for them."

14. Think aloud in front of your students. Let them hear you thinking, even better, puzzling your way slowly through problems in the subject. (Try to think aloud at the level of a good student, not as a speedy professional. If your thinking is too advanced or proceeds too quickly, they will not be able to internalize it.)

15. Regularly question your students Socratically: probing various dimensions of their thinking: their purpose, their evidence, reasons, data, their claims, beliefs, interpretations, deductions, conclusions, the implications and consequences of their thought, their response to alternative thinking from contrasting points of view, and so on.

16. Use concrete examples whenever you can to illustrate abstract concepts and thinking. Cite experiences that you believe are more or less common in the lives of your students (relevant to what you are teaching).